THE INSTANT
JUGGLING
BOOK

THE INSTANT JUGGLING BOOK

BOB WOODBURN

ILLUSTRATED BY KAREN LIOTA

WOODBURN LIFE BALANCE ASSOCIATES INC.

ISBN 0-9694324-0-2

Distribution by: FIREFLY BOOKS LTD.
3680 Victoria Park Avenue,
Willowdale, Ontario, Canada
M2H 3K1

Printed and bound in Canada
Juggling Cubes made in China (non-toxic using recycled plastic beads)

TABLE OF CONTENTS

Page

ACKNOWLEDGEMENTS 6

FORWARD 7

OPENERS 8

GETTING STARTED — BASIC BEGINNER JUGGLING 10

TRICKS, TRICKS, TRICKS

PART I — A "CHARACTER" BUILDER 18

PART II — A "PRETZEL" BUILDER 29

NOW REALLY . . . HAVEN'T YOU HAD ENOUGH? 73

THE LAST TOSS 74

RESOURCES 75

ABOUT THE AUTHOR 77

ACKNOWLEDGEMENTS

A warm and heartfelt thank you to some very special people whose loving support helped this book come alive —

- Karma and Jenna, my wonderful daughters;

- my family, friends, and unique clients who have been willing to try this and lots of other playful stuff; so I knew it would work.

You are truly a gift to me.

Bob Woodburn

FORWARD

One day, after my **MuchMusic** show, I was browsing in this neat games store, when I picked up a copy of Bob Woodburn's book. I discovered a terrific new passion, and a friend to boot.

It was great! I learned to juggle in one evening, and took my juggling cubes and new found skill to work the next day. Suddenly everyone in this off-beat place we affectionately call "the office" was juggling — on the air, off camera (except for the odd wild throw), behind the scenes . . . everywhere . . . all day long — in spite of work. We eventually even got Bob involved and did a show on it. It really was fun and very therapeutic.

There is a certain irony that real live juggling would catch on so well here at Citytv where we are all constantly juggling people, time and schedules anyway. Now we juggle for fun and relaxation too, all thanks to my friend Bob.

So check out the **Instant Juggling Book.** It's perfect! Anything that can provide this much fun and frolic for me and this intense crew — can do the same for you and yours. **It's an excellent adventure.**

Mike Rhodes
Citytv / MuchMusic
Host of Mike and Mike's Excellent X-Canada Adventures.

OPENERS

Aha! Caught ya! I'll bet you've already picked up the cubes and launched them in the air (or maybe into the bathtub). Congratulations! You've just joined an adventuresome and fast growing group of folks who have decided to try out this crazy world of identified (sometimes) and disappearing (often) flying objects.

Learning to juggle seems like it's supposed to be hard, but it's **NOT**. It's actually a piece of cake! My daughters got it when they were 8 and 9 years old; mom when she was 62; my uncoordinated friend at 34, just as he reached the peak of his awkwardness. AND SO WILL YOU!

How This All Got Started

So there I am, with a good friend in the Colorado Outward Bound School offices in Denver. "Want to juggle?" he says, and I respond decisively, "Maybe?" And he says, "Got a surefire way to teach you in 10 minutes. You'll be amazed at how amazing you can be." (Outward Bounders always say that kind of stuff).

It was really fun. We laughed and played like kids, and relaxed totally for those few minutes, and I got it. Then I was hooked, and wanted to do more. So I jumped in with both feet, and introduced it the very next week at a team-building seminar I was doing with a group of business executives. I used potatoes, cut in half, and even though it made an awful mess, they loved it, and also learned very quickly. I continued to do this with a number of other groups, and they all said the same thing: "This is great. You should get everyone to try this." So I thought, "Why not?", and created JUGGLE·EZ®. It's a "how-to" kit with a shorter book and three cubes, that was sold in game stores right across Canada and the United States. It had a great response and lots of people asked for more! So the **INSTANT JUGGLING BOOK** was born.

Benefits and Uncontrollable Urges

Sometimes the urge to teach juggling hits me in pretty unusual and exotic places: for instance, on a cable car in San Francisco; or a mountaintop at 13,000 feet in Banff, Alberta; or on a nude beach in Greece (now that's risky juggling). It's always fun and great to see people's reactions. Lee Fraser, a consultant and busy mother of two, said it as well as anybody: "I can't believe how fast I got this. I love it! It gives me a break from what I've been thinking about all day, and lets me forget about the world."

From my standpoint, that alone is a fabulous benefit. But there's more. It's also great for hand-eye coordination, for sharing with friends, for exercise, and for your soul, especially if done to music. SO RELAX, LIGHTEN-UP AND HAVE A BALL PLAYING WITH THIS.

BASIC BEGINNER JUGGLING — 3 STEPS TO SUCCESS

STEP 1

Pick up one cube.

★ Let it lie easily in the centre of your hand.

★ Stand comfortably with feet apart, knees slightly flexed and elbows bent at your side.

★ Have good light. Blackout juggling is supposed to be for **much** later.

★ Toss the cube lightly from one hand to the other — pause — then toss it back (in an arc about eye height). Do this over and over left to right — pause — right to left and repeat. **Don't rush.** Take your time.

★ Let the cube "**plop**" into the centre of your hand and keep your eye on it.

★ Try to keep all the throws the same.

★ Counting — say the number "1" out loud **as you let the cube go** (not after you release it).

★ Relax — **slow down.**

★ Practice this step for about 30 seconds or until it feels comfortable. Follow the cube's arc with your eyes all the way each time. **Don't transfer** the cube straight across. It must go **up and over.**

★ Note how well you're doing. See how all that "hidden" talent is just screaming to come out!

STEP 2

Place a cube in each hand.

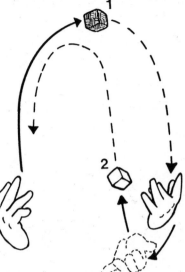

★ Toss the 1st cube up and over as in Step 1.

★ Just as the 1st cube reaches the top of its arc (eye level), toss the 2nd cube up and **under** the first one. Always look **up** at the cubes as much as possible.

★ **Swing** your hand toward the inside and send the 2nd cube straight up the centre line of your body (see illustration).

★ Don't pass the 2nd cube straight across from one hand to the other. **Each cube must go up and over.** Timing is everything. As you toss the 1st cube up, say "1". As soon as you **finish** saying "one", toss the 2nd cube up and say, "2". **Catch each cube in turn and stop!** Repeat this a number of times.

★ Note which hand you like to start with. That will be your "**dominant**" hand for the "Basic Start Position" talked about later.

★ If you find yourself **passing** or handing the cube straight across rather than sending it up and over... try starting with the non-dominant hand first to break that nasty habit immediately. Then return to a dominant hand start and try it again. You may end up being most comfortable starting with the non-dominant hand every time.

★ And finally, avoid the heartbreak associated with "cube smash" and "eyeball-split" from throwing both cubes at the same time. Read **Juggle Jive** (p. 13) for more tips and come out from the closet where you've been hiding and practicing. You'll need more room now.

STEP 3

Take the **Basic Start position** which is always the same ie. holding two cubes in your dominant hand (the hand you usually start with) and one cube in the other hand.

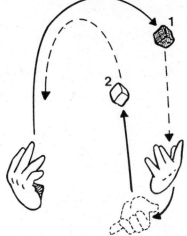

★ Start by tossing **only two** cubes as you did in Step 2. **Hold the extra cube back** in the heel of your hand. Start with the front cube of the hand that is holding two. Practise tossing just the two cubes back and forth and count 1...2...**Stop after each complete tossing of two cubes** the same as in Step 2. The one in the heel of your hand is **not** used yet — just held.

★ Now — **stretch** your counting to 1...2...3... and **anticipate** tossing the 3rd cube up. As soon as you finish saying "2", think about tossing the 3rd cube and say, "3" and move your hand as if you are going to send it — but don't let it go yet. Try that "fake" move twice.

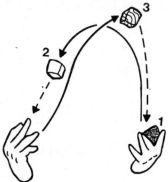

★ Now try all the cubes for the first time. Throw all three cubes 1...2...3...and **don't** try and catch any of them (this should be easy for you by now). Listen to the rhythm as they hit the floor. It should be even.

★ Then try and catch as many as you can. You may grab one or none. Don't worry — just keep trying.

★ Folks usually hang on to #3 too long. So now try sending the 3rd cube sooner by counting 1...2.3 (tossing 3 **right after** you finish saying "2"). **Remember** — every time you send a cube you say a number **immediately!**

★ Your brand new talent may be seeming quite hidden again (lost even?) It's okay. Remember your first tricycle ride? You just need more practice.

12

"JUGGLE JIVE" — EXTRA SPECIAL TIPS

★ Don't be discouraged if it takes longer than you expected. You have your own special pace, and its perfect!

★ Take breaks and keep trying.

★ Get someone to try it with you and help each other.

★ Relax. . .take your time and don't rush. By this time you know that your cubes like to play hide and seek a lot.

★ Watch the flight path of the cubes closely. Glue your eyes to the first one until it's halfway across, then switch and "eye in" the second (and third) cubes.

★ You probably should also know about the hazards of the frequent "Search and Rescue Operation". For example, if your piranha-filled aquarium is nearby and your "you know what" drops into "you know where". . .STOP! Or it will be far more challenging to juggle in the future.

★ Be deliberate. Try tossing the cubes a little higher and taking a bit more time between each throw and catch.

★ Slow down and count. 1...2...3..., NOT 1...2.3

★ Try it from a kneeling or praying position (we'll take all the help we can get), on a rug, or standing over a bed. It's easier to retrieve the cubes.
Remember to take a break and come back to it.

★ If you're reaching — it's OK! Everyone does. Try **over-compensating** and make the cubes curl back towards you. Try it a foot or so away from a smooth wall.

★ Carry your cubes everywhere and practice any time you can (maybe not while driving or standing at the edge of a cliff...!) And remember... **YOU CAN DO IT!** Persevere and enjoy!

14

CONTINUOUS JUGGLING — GOING FOR IT!

Do the same as Step 3. Then begin to **anticipate** making the 4th toss in a row the same as you did with the 3rd. Note which hand the 4th cube is coming from. Count 1...2...3...4... Force yourself to try it. **Don't worry about catching the cubes.** After four tosses, stop! Do that a number of times. Then, don't stop. Just keep tossing (and counting) as many times as you can (5...6...7 etc) Now...you've got it! **This is called the "cascade" pattern.**

The Cascade

It is actually the most basic juggling pattern and the favourite linking move for jugglers. Most tricks start from the cascade and return to it before going straight on to the next trick. So now you know the basic start and cascade moves. We will refer to these two a great deal in the next pages of tricks. Believe it or not, you will soon be building a "mini-routine" that will get you invited to lots of odd places or at least have you flying creatively around your home.

CONGRATULATIONS! YOU'RE NOW A TRUE JUGGLER AND ARE ON YOUR WAY TO FAME, FORTUNE AND A BRAND NEW OBSESSION! YOU DON'T BELIEVE ME?

READ ON!!!

TRICKS!

TRICKS!

TRICKS!

TRICKINESS PART I — A "CHARACTER" BUILDER

So now that you've perfected it all, sort of —
and are primed and ready for new challenges
and adventures of the spirit.

We delight in offering a variety of tricks for your enlightenment. You don't have to be
juggling great to try at least the first few tricks. They are designed to give you
the basic skills you need to carry this creative craziness on to other cosmic (or comic)
dimensions. All you have to do is be a little weird and have faith. You will soon
be impressing your friends with your skill and "trickiness". Start with the three
"tricky tips" below.

SOME IMPORTANT TRICKY TIPS

TIP #1

"Look Ma, I'm juggling!" It's essential
that you can complete at least 8
consecutive throws and catches,
preferably without sprinting flat out
all over the room.

We applaud your new fitness program,
however, its not so good for the
furniture (or your body). In spite of
what you may now believe, juggling is
not a contact sport.

TIP #2

As you do your cascade juggling (it's a figure eight pattern), imagine the cubes are inside an invisible glass frame suspended in front of you.

Attention sprinters and lungers: practice in front of a solid wall, not on your apartment balcony. It will help you be "trickier" faster (and stay that way longer).

TIP #3

There are often two methods shown for trying the tricks: (i) by counting 1...2...3 and (ii) by colour of cubes. Always try both ways to see which suits you best and don't forget ... this is a great way to terrorize supermarket managers!

SEMI-RIGID RULE

Do the first six tricks, in order, **before** you jump ahead. They will give you a solid base to build on. From that point, the tricks are generally in order of difficulty, but there's no hard and fast rule here. Follow your heart, be adventuresome and enjoy "rut-free" juggling. That is, if you get stuck in a trick, give it your best shot and then move on. Try others and come back to it later!

SKY HIGH

1. Take the **Basic Start** position.

*Note the colour of the single cube (e.g., red or it can be any colour you choose). It is always shown as the **key** one when doing tricks.

We have shown it as this design in most illustrations.

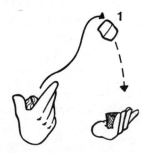

2. Start by tossing the first cube up the same as usual in your cascade pattern and say "1".

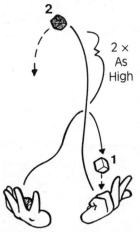

3. Now send the second cube (red) up **twice** as high as usual (say "2" **louder** as you do it).

4. Wait **patiently** for it to come down close to your opposite hand, then send the third cube **(call it "1" again)** up and over at the regular height.

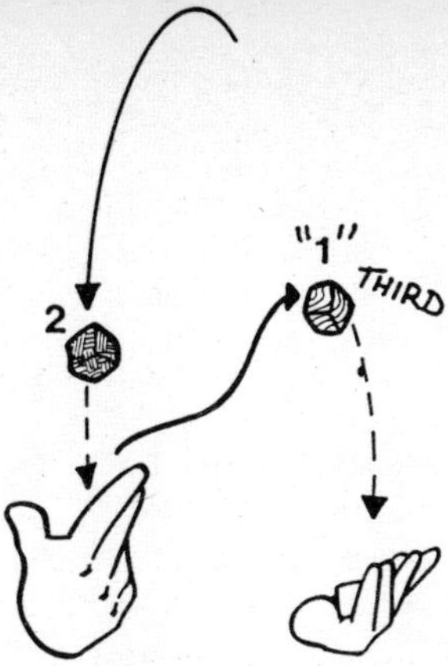

"1"
2
THIRD

5. Continue juggling 1...2... (you're still counting) sending the number 3 cube up (it's now the red one)

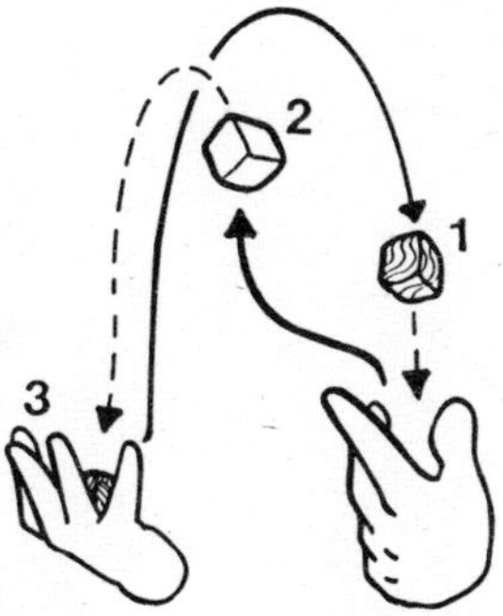

2
1
3

6. **Sky high** again. Note that it comes from the opposite hand. From then on every 3rd (red) cube (keep counting) will be tossed twice as high and be sent from alternating hands.

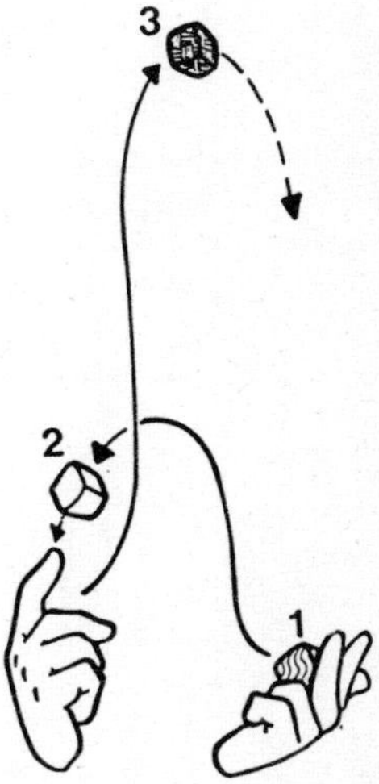

3
2
1

TRICKY TIP

★ Eventually you can throw a "sky high" anytime for a pattern break or to give you more time to set up for another trick.

THE BUMP 'N GRIND

1. Start by tossing a single cube a bit higher than usual straight up. Try a bump off one knee to find the right spot and height to catch the cube. Do this a number of times.

2. Always keep your eye on the cube all the way down until it hits your knee...

3. ...and all the way back up to catch it in the same hand as you sent it from. Once you get used to this, pick up three cubes and begin your normal cascade juggling.

4. Then, **every once in a while**, whenever you feel ready, **as you're juggling along**, bounce one of the cubes off your knee, catch it, continue juggling, bump it again, etc. Repeat this as often as you wish. Eventually try bouncing a cube off an extended foot (or other interesting part of your anatomy). (See "Things That Go Bump on Your Bod", p. 33)

THE WATER WORKS

1. Take the **Basic Start** position.

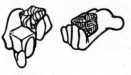

2. The Two Cube Fountain
Start juggling just the two cubes in your dominant hand for three rounds (1-2, 1-2, 1-2) in a fountain pattern above your hand.

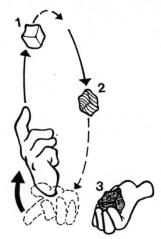

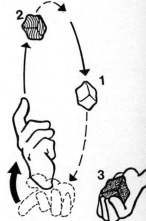

3. And then introduce the 3rd (single) cube up into the middle of the other two continuing right into

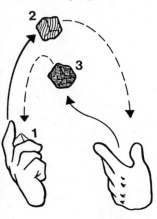

4. Your normal three cube cascade pattern. "Look Ma! Tricks!!"

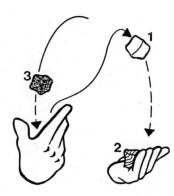

TRICKY TIPS

★ To get consistent height — imagine a spot above your head where the cubes should travel up to and try to hit it each time.

★ For a change, try starting the waterworks with two cubes in your **non-dominant** hand (try this with all your tricks eventually).

★ Later, you will see other different ways to do two cubes with both hands.

OVER THE RAINBOW

1. Picture a mini-rainbow in front of your eyes going from one hand to the other up over the top of your head.

2. Start with just **one** cube sending it in a rainbow arc above your head to the other hand. Move your hands out a bit wider and send it back and forth a number of times from hand to hand.

3. Now take the **Basic Start** position.

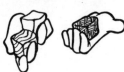

4. The first cube is sent up in the normal cascade pattern. The **second cube** however, goes outside. . .

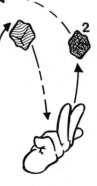

TRICKY TIP

★ It's tough to do this move continuously so. . .make **three outside passes in a row** and then switch right into your cascade before the next trick. This is how you build a continuous juggling routine (but don't give up your day job yet!)

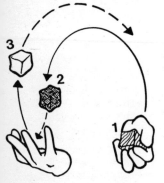

5. . . .and then the very next (3rd) cube and **every** cube from that point goes outside the cube coming down. Make your throws "soft".

THE GLITZY START

This is a fancy-looking move that looks harder than it is.

1. Take the **Basic Start** position and

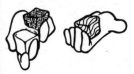

adapt it. The two cubes in your one hand are placed so that the front cube is held up between your thumb and forefinger while the back one is pressed in the heel of your hand with your little finger.

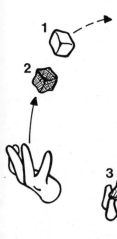

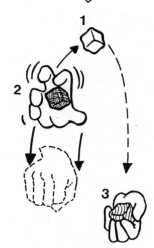

2. Send the two that are in your dominant hand up **at the same time**. Make sure that the one in the front of your hand goes higher than the other. Use a pointing up motion, ending with your fingers stretching towards the sky as you release the two cubes at the same time.

3. Immediately as they are still going up (before they reach their peak) grab the lower one with a clawing, swoop-down motion with the same hand as you sent them up with.

4. Then as the higher cube comes down to be exchanged with the cube in your **other** hand, continue into your normal cascade juggling pattern, getting ready for your next great trick.

THE FLASHY FINISH — TWIST AND SHOUT

1. Carry on juggling in your normal cascade pattern. Then throw the last cube that you want to finish with **very high**, curling it back towards you a bit.

2. Move under it, keeping your eyes on the cube **as long as you can**.

3. Reach your arm way around your back while stepping one foot forward and doing a 1/2 twist with your body towards the cube.

4. Catch it! Throw up your arms and shout whatever obscure and humble phrase comes to mind like FABULOUS! WOW! I **DID** IT!

5. Bow appropriately and keep smiling!

GOING FURTHER...DON'T STOP HERE!

★ Try juggling with different objects. High class restaurants are always impressed when their crystal begins to levitate.

★ Come out of the closet and go public. Juggle at your next big party but be cool about it. Just casually raid the fruit or bun bowl and do it. No announcements. A crowd will gather and your fame will spread (be prepared to replace the fruit depending on the degree of friendship you had with your hosts).

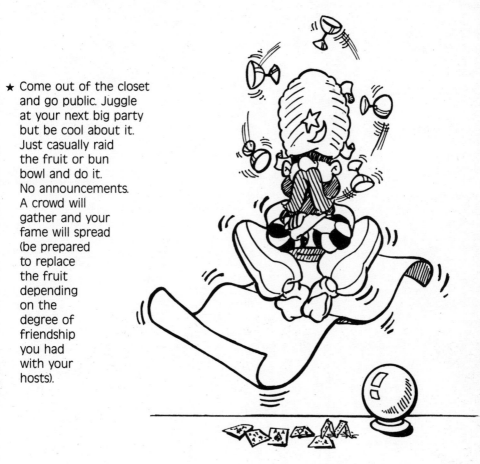

There's a whole world of possibilities out there waiting to be juggled. You can see it as either a fresh challenge or a new way to drive yourself crazy. Whatever turns you on!

NOW, TO FURTHER REDISCOVER YOUR TRUE CAPACITY FOR HUMILITY, READ AHEAD!!!

TRICKINESS PART II — A "PRETZEL" BUILDER

(Guess Who Becomes the Pretzel?)

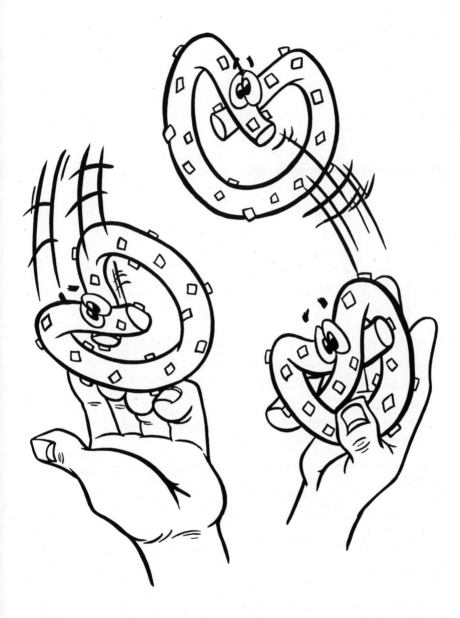

1. Take the Basic Start position. You will be using a two-step process to learn this simple and fun alternative to cascade juggling. It will help develop more handspeed, accuracy and precision.

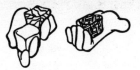

2. Start by tossing the first cube twice as high as usual from your dominant hand (aim at an imaginary point and try to hit it with each cube). Say "1" as you let it go (the same as in the Sky High).

As the first cube reaches the top of its arc, toss the second cube up and say "2".

3. Immediately, as you say "2", pass the third cube across to your dominant hand,

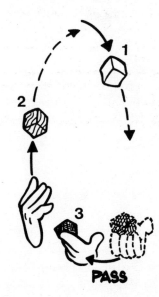

PASS

and catch cube 1 and then 2 in your non-dominant hand. Stop there. Do this at least twice successfully (meaning you hang onto all of the cubes).

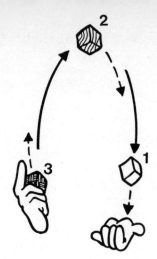

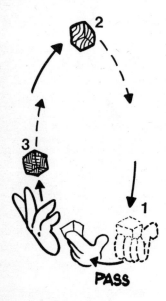

PASS

4. Now keep the shower pattern going continuously. Start, throw 1, then 2, quick-pass 3 across into your dominant hand and send it up immediately in your same nice high arc again. Catch cube 1 in your subordinate hand and pass it across; then send it up again immediately etc.

TRICKY TIP

★ As you get better at this move — you can speed up your hands, lower the arc and get very tight and controlled with your pattern.

THINGS THAT GO BUMP ON YOUR "BOD"

You've already got the first one in this series **The Bump 'n Grind** (pg. 22) shown below. We'll just take you further here.

1. Take the Basic Start position.

2. Send just one cube up and bump it off your knee. Do this three times, catching it each time.

Then toss the first cube up, bump it off your knee, and go right into your cascade juggling.

3. Finally, as you do your basic cascade, throw one cube up and bump it, then continue right on with your cascade. Bump again, continue on, etc.

Now you're ready to try other exotic bod parts.

TRICKY TIP

★ Practice each move three times starting as before with only one cube in your dominant hand. Throw it a little higher than usual and bounce it off another interesting part of your anatomy. As soon as you have the idea, begin from the Basic Start position, sending up one cube, bouncing it and going right into the cascade for your next trick.

Forearm

Back of Hand

Elbow

Forehead

Volleyball Style

Toe
(**Tip** — Leg and foot s-t-r-e-t-c-h-e-d out)

Side of Foot

COSMIC CYLINDERS AND OTHER "INNER" TUBES

1. Take the Basic Start position.

2. Throw one cube from each hand at the same time with both going to the same height. Do this move five times.

★ TIP — Look up. Pick an imaginary spot to throw to and imagine the cubes are each going up inside their own clear glass cylinder.

3. Then as the two cubes reach the top of their cylinder, send the third one up the middle between them (in its own clear tube), also going to the same height.

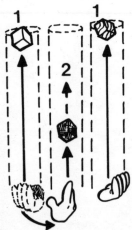

Catch the two coming down outside and **immediately** send them up again. Then catch the middle one that has just come down and send it up again. Repeat this pattern three times.

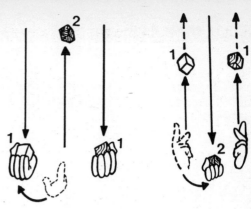

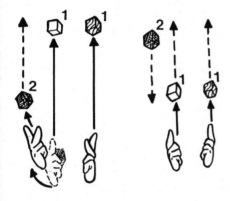

4. VARIATIONS

"**Going Up**". In the previous step the one in the middle has been "elevatored" there. Now you are going to move it out and over to the **right**. Repeat three times over there.

Now move the single cube over to the **left** side i.e. send two up in their cylinders, and as they peak, send the one on the left up in its own cylinder.

Do this three times.

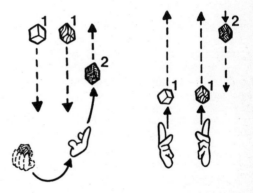

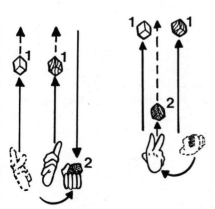

Singalong .. **Follow the Bouncing Cube**. Move the single cube into a new cylinder every second time it comes down without stopping in between moves. Start with the left, do it twice there, then move it into the middle twice, then over to the right twice. Then return to the cascade.

Cross Bend Cylinders

Start by sending the first two up and over so they bend towards the midline and cross at their peak.

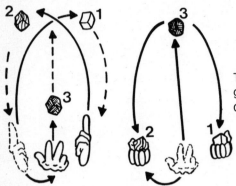

Then, without any pause, the single cube goes up in the middle. Stop when it comes down. Repeat this three times.

Now do the two cube bend followed immediately by the single cube up the middle. Repeat this two times without stopping, and then go immediately into your basic cascade and contemplate your next trick.

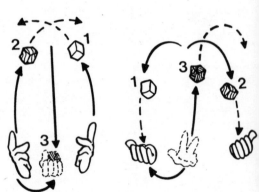

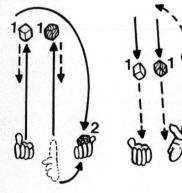

VolleyCube. Send two cubes up their cylinders, and then, as they start to come down, send the single third cube over the top of them both. Without stopping, repeat this action from the other side. Do this complete "volley" two times and then go into your cascade.

PUSH OVERS

1. Take the Basic Start position, but with your hands up (palms to ceiling and fingers pointing behind you), knees bent, upper body and head leaning back comfortably and looking up at the ceiling.

★ TIP: You will be pushing the cube up and **across**, so pick an imaginary spot to hit with each cube at its peak.

2. Follow exactly the same routine as you did to learn the basic **cascade technique**, except you are now juggling **above your head**. Reminder: Start with one cube, then do two and finally three. Then, without any stops, **push** the first cube up and **over**. As it reaches its peak, push the second up and over. As it peaks, push the third up and over, then stop.
Repeat this full step a few times.

3. Now don't stop. Keep going and do continuous juggling to a count of six cubes being exchanged, then come back down into the cascade and stop.

4. Now begin your pushover juggling right from the basic cascade. Start regular juggling, then throw one "Sky High". As it goes up, lean your head and body back and start your pushovers. Then after three passes, return to the cascade.

TRICKY TIPS

★ Try it to music. Could this be a "Cube-an" beat?
★ Dance while doing it
★ "Lazy Lobs" i.e. try doing it lying on your back (hammock juggling anyone?)

TWIST-TIME

1. Take the Basic Start position.

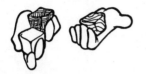

2. To begin juggling, raise your knee quickly and toss the first cube under that leg. Reach way under with your arm as you toss this cube up and over.

Then carry on with the cascade a bit. Stop. Do that combination twice more.

41

3. Now begin regular cascade juggling first. If you are right handed, do a "Sky High" from your right hand to buy some time, and then throw the next cube (also from your right hand) under your raised right leg and return to cascade juggling. Repeat this move three times.

TRICKY TIP

★ Do not start this one while standing at the edge of your neighbour's deck on the cliffs of Acapulco.

★ **OPTION:** (if right handed) Throw a high one from your right hand to buy time, and then do a right hander under your **left** leg. (This seems easier for some people).

THE FLASHBACK

1. Start with only one cube. Throw it behind your back with your dominant hand so that it curls up and over your shoulder. Catch it with your other hand at belt height.

Then throw it from that hand behind your back and over your other shoulder.

TIP — Look up to the side the cube is coming over, and as it appears and peaks, eye it in and get ready to send the next one. Make sure your back throws are consistent and always close to the same spot.

P.S. These challenging moves will take some practice but hey, as Ashleigh Brilliant so aptly put it — "If I don't do the things that are not worth doing, who will?"

2. Now take the Basic Start position and

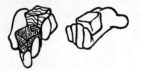

send the front cube (#1 of the two held in your dominant hand) over behind your back. As it appears above your shoulder, throw #2 over in front of you. As it peaks, throw #3 and begin your cascade juggling. Then stop. Repeat this step a number of times starting from alternate sides, i.e. start with two in your other, **non-dominant** hand and begin the move by throwing the first cube behind your back as before.

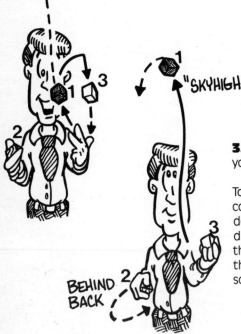

"SKYHIGH"

BEHIND BACK

3. Now do this "flash back" move while you are doing your cascade juggling pattern.

To start: As you do the cascade, pick a colour you will use. When it comes into your dominant (right) hand, (#2 cube in our diagram) **quickly** move it down to reach and throw behind your back. Remember to send the previous cube "Sky High" to buy some time.

4. Look for it over your shoulder, and **be patient** — it will likely show up. When it does just keep juggling. However, if it doesn't, you should look for it in the most obscure places that you're **positive** it couldn't be in.

BEHIND BACK

5. Use the same hand a number of times until you get it. Then try alternating with the other hand. Start slowly, using the same steps as before.

Suggestion:
To test your sanity further, try it with the opposite hand, over the other shoulder right from your cascade. Lead into it slowly with the same steps as before, i.e. cascade juggle, and then send it with that other hand.

TRICKY TIPS

★ If you get to this point, you may want to quit while you're ahead. However, if you truly feel "called" to go on, and are prepared to take early retirement (you'll need the time) go to the next step. It's "hot" and it's called the **Back Cross**. From your cascade, go behind the back with one hand, then immediately throw behind the back with the other one. Carry on with your cascade and then repeat.

★ Turn your head **quickly** to see the cubes as they come into view on one side and then the other.

CREATIVE COVERUPS ...
"HEY, IT'S ALL PART OF THE SHOW."

(For those **rare** occasions when one of your cubes has landed on the floor. . .)

1. "Roll your own." After the cube hits the floor, stop juggling and roll it casually onto your right toe with your left foot.

ROLL CUBE
ONTO OTHER
FOOT

FLIP UP

Kick it up, go **smoothly** into the cascade pattern and rap a bit for your attentive audience (probably the dog and cat). "Knew you'd love that planned part of the routine, but please, hold your applause."

2. "Kick up your heels!"

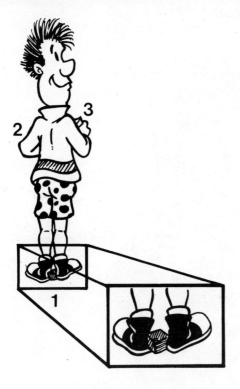

Send it up over your shoulder...

and continue juggling.

"MIRROR MIRROR ON THE WALL . . ."

1. Cascade juggle in front of your favourite looking glass. Don't look at the cubes directly, but see them (and yourself) in the mirror. Talk or sing to yourself. Practice this technique by focusing in on something **past** the cubes as often as possible when not in front of a mirror.

TRICKY TIP

★ Notice the cubes, especially at the top of their path, but don't **watch** them too closely.

THE PAUSE THAT REFRESHES (OR DRIVES YOU CRAZY)

(Don't forget it's all about being patient ... remember that?)

1. The Forearm (palm side up)

TIP: To absorb the cube, raise your arm straight up to **softly** meet the cube. Just before the cube hits, let your arm down with the same speed as the cube and **give** with it. Overdo this motion and "sink" your whole body (bend your knees and move down with the cube). Really concentrate by keeping your eyes focused on the cube all the way until it stays still on your arm then pause, flip it up and cascade again.

ARM MOVES DOWN AT THE SAME SPEED AS THE CUBE

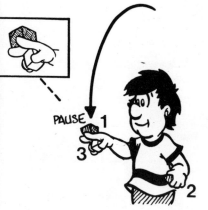

PAUSE 1
3

2. Jugglers speak with "forked" fingers.

Start your cascade juggle. Then send one "Sky High" and catch it by making a fork with your fingers. (the Kung Fu eye gouge position, invaluable in all slam juggling circles). Remember, let your hand move down and "give" under the cube.

Pause dramatically, then flip it back up in the air and claw down, grabbing it with the same hand, so that there are now two in your right hand.

3
FLIP UP
2

1 3
GRAB DOWN
2

1 3 2

Now, in a smooth motion, swing behind your back with the two cubes and toss the front one up over your opposite shoulder. Then exchange the one, toss #2 and go right into your cascade. Try it first with just one of the cubes being sent up over your shoulder; later send both cubes at once.

THROW BEHIND BACK

PAUSE

FLIP UP

3. A Flashy Option
Catch the cube in the fork of your fingers, again on the back of your hand.

Then really show off by raising your hand right back up, releasing both cubes straight up into the air.

Claw down on the **top** cube (#3) and bring your forked fingers under the lower one again (#1) as you hunker your whole body down to create a dramatic catch just before it hits the ground

GRAB TOP CUBE

GET UNDER CUBE 1 FAST!

THROW BEHIND BACK

Jump up gracefully and swing the two behind your back again, letting one go and recommencing cascade juggling.

4. Tender Toes

Move your foot down fast just as the cube is about to hit it. Pause. Smile. Flip it up and cascade again.

5. Neck Flips

Send a cube "Sky High". Watch it until the **last second**, then lean forward from your waist, keeping your back and neck straight, eyes looking up and ahead on the floor as far as you can. Catch the cube on the back of your neck. Pause. Tilt your head down slowly, let cube start to roll forward. As it does, snap your head up, sending the cube into the air so that you can restart cascade juggling.

TRICKY TIP

★ It really helps to put your arms straight out to the side or hands on your knees as you first bend forward.

6. "Off With His Head ..."

Unless your friends call you "flat head", practice a few times with one cube first, placing it on your head with your left hand very deliberately and firmly. Then try the trick. Send 1 higher with your right hand. Put 2 on your head (left hand) and catch 1 in your left hand.
Let 2 fall.

Throw 3 up under it and begin your cascade again.

7. The Scratch and Find

A ridiculous variation, but fun, and not too hard.

When you get slower and more controlled, (meaning the cube stays on your head until you tilt it off) try "The Scratch and Find". After you place the cube on your head with your left hand, reach up with your right hand and actually **take it off**. Continue your cascade, eventually "Scratching and Finding" every time! (for three passes)

THE GARDEN OF EDEN AND THE OLD APPLE TRICK

1. Take the Basic Start position, only with two cubes and an apple. The apple is in the front of your dominant hand, the cube in behind.

2. Start the cascade and count "..1 ...2 ...3 ...4 ...5", counting **each time** a cube goes. At "5", the apple is back in your dominant hand. Try this twice.

THE APPLE IS NOW "4"

53

3. Then do it again. This time, as you say "5", send the cube in your subordinate hand "Sky High". The apple is now in your dominant hand. At this point, when "5" is in the air, kiss the apple **quickly** (this is no time for romance). Do this a number of times.

4. Now **cascade**, and kiss the apple **each time** it hits your right hand. Remember, you have to be fast. Bring the apple up and quickly get it down and back into the cascade.

TRICKY TIP

5. Once you get the kiss down, try a cautious "mini-bite". Watch your upper plate. . . you can crunch your teeth here.

★ The sloppier and messier the technique the more most people (except your mom) will love it. Feel free to talk with your mouth full. (This is a great training exercise for budding politicians)

TRICKY TIPS

★ Every time the apple ends up in your right or dominant hand, send the other cube higher and bite the apple. Eventually, do it without sending the previous cube higher.

★ Be sophisticated. Try other kinds of weird and wonderful fruit — plums, cherries, olives (for martini lovers). Or how about Passion Fruit?

★ Create and tell your own unique "Garden of Eden" story as you do this trick. It's a big hit from neighbourhood pulpits.

PARTNERING (OR HOW TO END A BEAUTIFUL FRIENDSHIP)

TERRIFIC TAKE AWAYS

There are two variations of this. **Occasionally** taking the cube away each time you are ready; or taking it **every time**, so the cube goes back and forth rapidly between partners.

1. Closeness Counts:
Start off with the tips of your fingers just touching (ooooh, love that contact!) when you are both standing in the Basic Start position.

2. Your partner has the three cubes (you don't) and starts juggling, deliberately and as slowly as possible, sending the cubes a little higher than normal. You watch closely, concentrating very hard and following the flight of the cubes. (Your eyes and brain love not cooperating on this one!)

TIP — Your partner must continue juggling, no matter what (a lot of strange things can happen here) until you TAKE all three cubes.

3. As your partner does a continuous cascade, watch closely. Then as soon as a cube starts to come out of your partner's **right** hand, you will reach immediately **across and in** with your right hand and grab the cube. It will be at the top of its arc by the time your brain says "go" and does it.

P — Reach in with your hand (thumb-up) s if you are going to grasp a vertical pole. rab at the cube sideways with your palm.

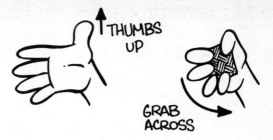

THUMBS UP

GRAB ACROSS

4. After you grab the one cube, **immediately** reach across the other side with your left hand and grab the cube now coming out of your partner's left hand.

5. Now ... a mini-pause. Then as you stand with one cube in each hand, your partner has let the third cube go up. You take over to that as the third one peaks, you introduce it into your cascade — shouting some dramatic phrase like "Holy Cow ... We did it!" (whereupon you usually drop all the cubes, saying some other dramatic phrase like "Holy ————!").

6. Now your partner repeats the above five steps and takes the three cubes from you. "Takes" is the key word — you **keep juggling** until they are all gone — no matter what!

7. Once you "get it", then try and take the cubes continuously, every time, so that each person does one cascade, the cubes are gone, then they **immediately** take them back, etc.

57

SIDE "SWIPES"

1. Stand side by side.

2. The partner on the left begins to cascade juggle three cubes. You reach high into the middle with your **left** hand and take the cube that comes from your partner's **right** hand **at its peak.**

3. Then immediately you reach across your partner's face (this is where it pays to be good friends). Take the cube that has just come out of his/her left hand. At this point, you have one cube in each hand.

4. As you now move deliberately in front of him, be patient as your partner sends the third cube up towards the midline of your body (between your hands). As it peaks, send the first cube from your left hand and begin juggling so there is no break from your partner's cascade to yours.

5. Your partner steps back and around behind you (as you continue to cascade), then steps forward and does the **takeover** the same way you did.

PASSING — also known as "Three Cube Chaos"

This exercise is so much fun and you have such a great feeling from "getting it", that it is worth the effort. As my friend Bill Oliver and I decided one hot summer's day, while he was trying to teach me this move, beer helps. For all you underage jugglers, any other beverage is just as good . . . trust me!

1. Both partners have three cubes (two in the right hand and one in the left), and are ready to juggle.

Stand opposite each other, about seven feet apart and hold your **hands up at eye level.**

One person says "ready **and** go". On "go", you both smoothly drop your hands down to the Basic Start position and immediately begin cascade juggling.

DROP HANDS AND JUGGLE

|— 7' —|
2.5 METERS

2. Look **through** your pattern to "see" your partner's pattern while noticing (but not watching closely), your own. Get in sync. It is important that both sets of cubes are being juggled at roughly the same speed and height. You want to have the same tempo.

Do this pre-passing exercise by counting "1 and 2 and 3 and throw", "and 1 and 2 and 3 and throw" (don't actually throw the cube yet). You say a number or an "and" **every** time you send a cube up in

your cascade. Repeat this cycle three times, **stopping** after you say "throw" each time. Make sure that your timing is the same. For example, does the last cube land in your respective hands at the same time?

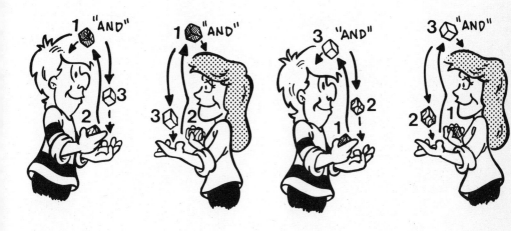

(Oh, by the way, this can end a lovely friendship right here, so you should decide how obsessive you are about   a) the friendship; b) the juggling; c) the three cube passing; d) any or all of the above.)

3. The Real Thing

Once you get this reasonably well (honest, it doesn't take very long for most of us "profoundly average" folks), then you are ready for the real thing.

Look back at Step 1. Face each other, seven feet apart, and begin the same as you did initially (Step 1), only you will now throw to each other. Count "1 and 2 and 3 and", throwing it straight across on the "**and**" after 3.

Concentrate on sending it accurately up and over, straight across to your partner's **left** hand from your right.

TIP — Slow down! Make your throws across a little higher and lazier. Do this a number of times. In other words, continue "1 and 2 and 3 and throw" until it feels comfortable. Drink more beer/lemonade.

4. Catch with your left hand and continue cascade juggling, counting "1 **and** 2 **and** 3 **and**." Remember to say "1" **as you receive** the incoming cube in your left hand from your partner.

Do this pass (i.e. sending a cube across) three times, then stop. At this point it's critical to shout "WOW" or "Right on" or some other deeply spiritual message to celebrate this amazing event.

THE BIG TRICKY TIP

★ Psssst. Want to know the BIG secret? It's found in the numbers "3-3-10".

When you see pro jugglers do this routine with clubs, hats, knives and other items of extreme craziness, their secret is 3-3-10. The way it works is that each **THIRD** cube (thrown on "3 **and**") goes over to your partner **three times**. Then you switch so that every **SECOND** cube i.e. "1 and 2 **and**" is sent across from your right to his left (also **three times**). Then **EVERY** cube that lands in your right hand is passed across **ten** times and then you stop. It looks like this:

"Ready and go"
1 and 2 and 3 and **send**╱ 3X
1 and 2 and **send**╱ 3X
1 and **send**╱ 10X

On this last round count — "1 and 2 and 3 and 4" etc. (up to 10), sending a cube each time you say an "**and**".

TRICKY TIP

★ **Ah ah, I see the light.**
(You do?) Imagine that there is a cosmic clothesline or a ray of light zapping straight across between your hands and your partner's hands. The cube will then arc high over on that path.

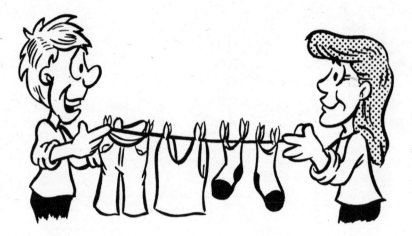

FOUR CUBES ARE YOU CRAZY?

Ok! Ok! If you insist, we'll get you started.

As you can see from the illustration, there's a slight chance you'll experience some mild frustration while taking your next vacation to master this. But we understand. At this point, you've got to go-for-it . . . Right!

FOUR CUBES

First of all, you need to work on each hand independently.

1. Remember what you did for the two cube fountain (p. 15). Do that three times. with one hand. Then do it with the other hand.

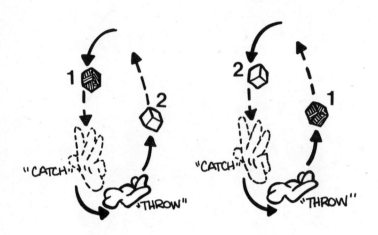

2. Reverse the fountain and send the cubes in the other direction. Again, do it first with one hand and then with the other. Note that your hand needs to swing into the midline and then your wrist flips or turns slightly towards the outside to send the cube up and out.

OH MY GOD, FOUR, USING BOTH HANDS AT ONCE!

3. TWO FROM EACH HAND — AT THE SAME TIME

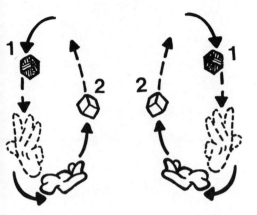

OUTERS

Hold two cubes in each hand. Send one cube simultaneously from each hand. As those cubes peak send the next two. Keep this identical rhythm pattern going without stopping. Do three passes.

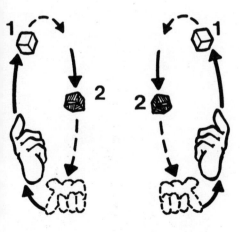

INNERS

The reverse (or perverse) of outers. Send the first two cubes. As they peak send the next two. Don't stop . . . ever!

4. TWO FROM EACH HAND AT DIFFERENT (ALTERNATING) TIMES

THE AC/DC MOVE

This creates the illusion that the cubes are crossing and that you're cascading four. They're not, and you're not. Each hand still works separately, only now on **different** rhythms. Counting does help here.

Start by saying "1" and send a cube; then immediately say "2" and send a cube quickly from the other hand. Then with no pause say "3" and send again from the 1st hand; and finally say "4", and send the last cube. Just do this cycle once, catch all the cubes (sure buddy!) and stop. Repeat the cycle three times. The cubes do not stray across the midline of your body.

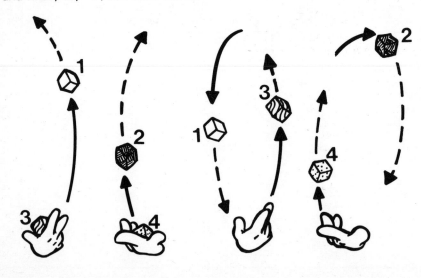

Then try it twice in succession:
1,2,3,4 — 1,2,3,4, and stop.

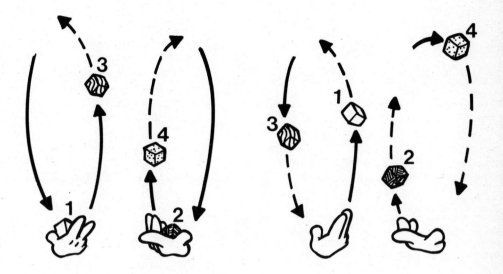

TRICKY TIP

★ If possible, use two cubes of the same colour in one hand and two of another colour in the opposite hand so you can pick up "strays" as they sneak over into the other hand (a "no no" in this trick).

★ Once you get two rounds in succession, then go for more rounds to help you get quicker and smoother with this.

CLUBS AND OTHER PARAPHERNALIA (YOU ARE CRAZY!)

So now you wanna juggle chain saws, bicycles, clubs, exam schedules, the "books" and other strange and exotic items. (I have a friend who juggles a cross-country ski, a ping pong ball and a tennis racquet. He's obviously improving his athletic scope and prowess but we all agree he's weird man). I guess if you've come this far — you also qualify as weird enough to do this.

I **assume** you've already tried other **smaller,** more friendly objects like tennis or lacrosse balls. If not, do them first. They are fun and present all kinds of new possibilities to "bounce" and expand your juggling horizons. **Before** you move on to other exotic flying apparatus read the **BIG TIPS** that follow.

BIG TIP #1:

Start with **clubs — Please!** Soft, light clubs that are especially made for this. Contact the folks referred to in the back of this book under **Resources** to get them. We don't recommend that anyone try to juggle any of the sharp and dangerous stuff — leave it for the pros.

BIG TIP #2:

Get "**The Complete Juggler**" by Dave Finnigan (Vintage Books). This is a great, very comprehensive book, put together by a man who has dedicated himself to teaching others the art of juggling. Lots of terrific club and other advanced stuff in here.

BIG TIP #3:

Join a juggling group — like the Toronto Jugglers' Club — there is one in almost every major urban area . . . and help "heal" each other of your upcoming bruises or this new-found multi-objects obsession. If there isn't a group in your city, start one. What the heck, anyone obsessed enough to go this far can bring that off easy.

BIG TIP #4:

Say goodbye to your best antique furniture and **GO FOR IT!**

BIG TIP #5

Have a good Doc who understands "jugglemania".

NOW REALLY ... HAVEN'T YOU HAD ENOUGH?

This is as far as I can go before I lose all my friends who helped field test this book. I'm sure you know what I mean as your friends tire of being "partners" again and of hearing the beloved thump, thud, crash and sweet (?#$!!*!!) words of a newly "possessed" juggler.

If you've tried most of the stuff in here, you're probably really hooked by now ... CONGRATULATIONS! You've got an edge on a new passion that will enliven your spirit and give you much satisfaction for the rest of your life.

GOOD LUCK! AND HAPPY JUGGLING!

THE LAST TOSS...

How about creating a Juggling "happening" to share with your business associates and friends. I love doing these events with large or small groups as this recent **Business Journal** article shows.

CITY BUSINESS

Corporate Jester

BOB WOODBURN has come up with one wacky ice-breaker for his lifestyle management workshops: picture, if you will, 500 executives attired in their boardroom best, standing cheek by jowl, juggling cloth cubes.

There is method in this madness. Woodburn who runs a consulting business, **Rethink Inc.**, says juggling allows him "an entree with a group to talk about how they're juggling too many things in their life, or the wrong kinds of things."

He says juggling also makes people who are in a rut realize that the only way to get out is to try something new. "And, in order to try something new," he says, "we've got to be willing to look a little foolish."

Five years after adding the juggling twist to life-style lectures, Woodburn estimates that he has taught 8,000 people to juggle.

Woodburn's stock-in-trade has been a great equalizer for such orga-nizations as **Canada Life** and **McKinsey & Company**, which brought together people from various levels to learn to juggle.

Why do companies pay Woodburn to teach employees to juggle? Because, like magic, zen, or sex, says Woodburn, juggling is a great mind relaxant. "You can't think of anything else while you're doing it". Juggling instruction is followed by a lecture on lifestyle management, or in the executive workshops, exercises and role playing to determine an executive's lifestyle balance requirements.

by Cynthia Macdonald

If you or your organization are interested in a workshop or a conference session contact me through my distributor.

CONTACTS AND RESOURCES

JUGGLING CLUBS/ORGANIZATIONS

The International Jugglers Association (IJA)

This 3,000 member "family" is a great place to start to expand your juggling interests. Membership includes a fine quarterly journal, **Jugglers World**, that lets you know what's going on in the world of juggling, plus some great stories, tips and contacts such as the list of many local clubs in Canada and the United States. They also have a terrific annual conference.

IJA P.O. Box 29, Kenmore, New York 14217 USA
  (716) 876-5331

Local Clubs

Most major cities have one. Ask around, especially of local performing jugglers, or start your own.

EQUIPMENT

To get your hands on some good juggling supplies by mail there are a number of companies who advertise in **Jugglers World** (the IJA journal). Otherwise visit your local kite, toy, magic or sporting goods store. If all else fails contact us. We can supply more juggling cubes and direct you to other air borne goodies.

MAGAZINES

Juggler's World. This quarterly magazine puts the most comprehensive information on the field together in a neat package. Learn new tricks for your act, find out who's hot, where festivals are held and read about the rich history of this dynamic variety art.

Contact: IJA: Box 29
          Kenmore, NY 14217

Kaskade. Savor the colorful juggling scene in Europe. There are stories on groups, performances, reviews of books and shows, a workshop section and more! For a year's subscription send a $10 bill to:

Gabi & Paul Keast
Annastr. 7
D-6200 Wiesbaden
W. Germany